The Heart of R

David Farr is a writer and directo _ _ _ _ _ _ _ _ _ _ *The Danny Crowe Show*, *Elton John's Glasses*, *Night of the Soul*, *The UN Inspector* and a collection of adaptations have all been published by Faber. He was Artistic Director of London's Gate Theatre from 1995 to 1998, and Joint Artistic Director of Bristol Old Vic from 2002 to 2005. He has directed *Coriolanus* and *Julius Caesar* for the Royal Shakespeare Company and *The UN Inspector* for the National Theatre. In June 2005 he became Artistic Director of the Lyric Theatre, Hammersmith, where his productions included new versions of *The Odyssey* and Kafka's *Metamorphosis*. In 2009 he became Associate Director of the RSC, where his productions of *The Winter's Tale*, *King Lear* and *The Homecoming* opened to critical acclaim.

DAVID FARR

The Heart of Robin Hood

faber and faber

First published in 2011
by Faber and Faber Limited
74–77 Great Russell Street, London WC1B 3DA

Typeset by Country Setting, Kingsdown, Kent CT14 8ES
Printed in England by CPI Group (UK) Ltd, Croydon CR0 4YY

A CIP record for this book
is available from the British Library

ISBN 978–0–571–28355–2

2 4 6 8 10 9 7 5 3 1

For Bessie and Claudie Farr,
my own Marions

*I would like to thank Gisli Örn Gardarsson
and Börkur Jonsson for their collaboration
on the first production*

The Heart of Robin Hood was first performed by the Royal Shakespeare Company in the Royal Shakespeare Theatre, Stratford-upon-Avon, on 18 November 2011. The cast was as follows:

Lord Falconbury Gareth Aled
Plug the Dog Peter Bray
Prince John Martin Hutson
Rebecca Summers / Lady Falconbury Fiona Lait
Much Róbert Lučkay
Margaret LeBrun / Green Man Emma Manton
Robin Hood James McArdle
Alice Flora Montgomery
Pierre Ólafur Darri Ólafsson
Marion Iris Roberts
Will Darwin Shaw
Guy of Gisborne / Duke of York / George LeBrun
  Tim Treloar
Little John Michael Walter
Robert Summers / Friar Marcello Walton
Makepeace Lawrence Werber
Gisborne's Henchman Addis Williams
Jethro Summers Bailey Fear, Jack Firth, Tom Ransford
Sarah Summers Heather Croghan-Miksch, Isabelle Evans,
  Molly Pipe

All other parts played by members of the Company.

This text may differ slightly from the play as performed.

Directed by Gisli Örn Gardarsson
Designed by Börkur Jonsson
Costume designed by Emma Ryott
Lighting designed by Björn Helgason
Music by Högni Egilsson
Sound designed by Gregory Clarke
Associate Director and Movement by Selma Björnsdóttir
Fights by Kev McCurdy
Company Dramaturg Jeanie O'Hare
Company Text and Voice Work by Stephen Kemble
Additional Company movement by Struan Leslie
Assistant Director Dan Coleman
Casting by Janine Snape CDG
Children's casting by Barbara Roberts CDG
Production Manager Simon Ash
Costume Supervisor Janet Bench
Company Manager Jondon
Stage Manager Pip Horobin
Deputy Stage Manager Gabrielle Sanders
Assistant Stage Manager Joanna Vimpany

*The RSC Ensemble is generously supported by the Gatsby
Charitable Foundation and the Kovner Foundation.*

*The RSC Literary Department is generously supported
by the Drue Heinz Trust.*

*The RSC is grateful for the significant support of its
principal funder, Arts Council England, without which
our work would not be possible. Around 50 per cent of
the RSC's income is self-generated from box-office sales,
sponsorship, donations, enterprise and partnerships with
other organisations.*

Supported by
**ARTS COUNCIL
ENGLAND**

Characters

Robin Hood
Will
Much
Little John
Marion
Alice
Pierre
Makepeace
Jethro
Sarah
Robert Summers
Prince John
Guy of Gisborne
Townspeople
Soldiers
Priests, Friars, Bishops
Aristocrats, Lords and Ladies
Duke of York
The Green Man

Setting

This piece is imagined broadly for a bare stage.
A tree may be worth exploring.

THE HEART OF ROBIN HOOD

Prologue

Pierre at the foot of an English oak, singing.

Pierre
    And when the swifts do come again
    From winter in the south

    And when the bluebell starts to spring
    Inside of April's mouth

    Will you come back to me, my love?
    Will you come back to me?

    And when the honey sun does melt
    The snow from on the path

    And when the honey sun does melt
    The ice from in my heart

    Will you come back to me, my love?
    Oh will you come back to . . .

Oh hello. You caught me in mid flow. My name's Pierre.
Once of the highest court of the Duke of York. Never
seen but in satin. Hair puffed like a fresh meringue. Not
any more. Looks? Vanity? Civilisation? Forget it. You see
before you a man of nature.
    The countryside. Try it. Countryside. Marvellous.
Just hear those birds.

    Bird song.

Wonderful.
    Yes, the leaves are back on the trees. It's spring again.
And here I am, a minor god of the greensward. Rural

3

man. Pastoral Pierre. The champain. Arcadia. Cheese.
Fish. Plums.

But how did I get here? Whence this remarkable
change?

The answer's up there.

In the oak. The English oak.

*He contemplates the oak. A carriage appears in the
mists of another time.*

How I found my heart.

And Robin Hood found his.

Act One

A storm. Thunder. Lightning. A carriage hurtling through the forest. A driver, Little John, cracks the whip on the horses as fast as he can.

Aristocrat Faster!

Wife Faster!

Little John This is as fast as I dare!

Aristocrat Call this fast?!

Wife Call yourself a horseman?!

Aristocrat We must be at York by dawn! We have letters for the Duke's court!

Little John I can't go faster in this storm, sir. This is Robin Hood country. We crash here, we come out with nothing!

Aristocrat Coward!

Wife Take the reins, George.

Aristocrat Give me the whip. I'll show you speed.

Little John These horses are newly broken, they won't take to roughness.

Wife Then why in heaven do we have new horses?

Little John Because the old ones died of your beatings.

Aristocrat Give me that whip!

Little John Your honour, please!

Wife Give it to him!

*The Aristocrat seizes the whip and reins and wildly
lashes the horses.*

Aristocrat I'll show you speed, you lackey! Ha! Ha! Ha!

*A crack of thunder. The horses panic and the carriage
suddenly turns, throwing the passengers. The horses
bolt into the forest.*

Our horses! Get them back!

Wife Call them.

Little John You call them.

Aristocrat They won't answer our call.

Little John Then run after them. I won't bring the poor
devils back to this misery.

Aristocrat You whoreson villain. You will pull the
carriage yourself.

He whips John.

Pull it. Pull it, lackey!

He whips him.

Wife Harder. Whip him harder.

*They whip Little John, but as they do so are slowly
surrounded by Robin Hood, Will Scathlock and Much
Miller in the trees around them.*

Robin One more lash on his back and I'll tear your skin
from your shoulders, hang it from this tree, dry it, cure
it, and use it as a gourd for my mead. And with every
swig I'll toast the raw flesh of its owner that I left alive
hanging for the crows to peck at, with the white breasts
of his lady there as soft sweet dumplings for afters. Your
choice.

Pause.

What is your name?

Aristocrat George LeBrun. Landowner.

Robin Where do you travel?

Aristocrat To the castle at York. I have letters of highest importance for the Duke's daughter. For which reason I demand you set us free!

Robin The Duke's daughter must of course receive her letters. Leave the carriage here. You may take them on foot.

Wife But the carriage . . . contains . . .

She stops herself.

Much Contains what?

Aristocrat Matters of the highest intelligence!

Robin Then you will have no objection to pulling it yourselves.

Wife How dare you?

Aristocrat Margaret. Do what the man says.

Robin Hood and his men tie the reins to the Aristocrats. They pull.

Will It won't move, chief.

Robin T-t-t-t. We must lose some weight from the carriage.

He takes out gold and silver from the carriage.

This gold and silver weighs you down.

Aristocrat That is my gold . . .

Robin What's gold compared to the letters you have for the Duke's daughter? Pull again.

They pull but to no avail. Robin takes furs and coins.

These furs are too weighty. Your path will be easier without them.

Wife But . . .

Robin What's fox and sable compared to the news you must carry to the castle?

They pull again. The carriage starts to move.

There, what did I say? It is scarce twenty miles to York. If you run you'll be there by sundown. Now go. Go! Ha! Ha! Ha!

He whips the ground and the Aristocrats pull the carriage away and into the forest.

This is our camp. Take rest a while.

Little John Thank you, sir.

Robin Your name?

Little John John Hardy, sir. Ostler.

Robin Robin Hood. Gangster.

Will Will Scathlock. Thief.

Much Much Miller. Liar, cheat and poet. In that order.

Robin Will you join us, Little John?

Little John stands.

Little John I will join you. For you cannot be bigger thieves than these I have served these last years.

Robin Read the oath, Will.

Will
Do you, John,
Swear to be faithful to the order of the oak,
To steal what you can steal,

To obey no law of God nor man,
To be free, under no king's orders,
No lord's edicts and no church's summons,
Only dancing to the music of your own soul
And the forest beneath your feet?

Little John I do.

Robin One more thing. Tell him.

Will Chief . . .

Robin Tell him.

Will Do you promise at no time to bring a woman into our company?

Little John What, never?

Will Never.

Much Ever.

Little John Why?

Robin A woman causes storms in the heart of man. This forest is our fortress. Make your heart one too.

Will Swear it.

Little John I swear.

Robin Follow us.

SCENE TWO

Two peasant children, rough clothes, playing in the fields. Distant thunder.

Jethro It's dawn in the forest. There's fairies in the trees. Can you see them? The Green Man in the oak. Hearne the Hunter smiling from the branches. They'll protect us, Sarah.

9

Sarah I can hear the fairies dancing. They're getting closer, Jethro.

Jethro listens.

Jethro That's no fairies.

They hide. They see a procession. Soldiers. Flags. And the King's brother's carriage, the occupants hidden by a covering.

Sarah Who was it, Jethro? Was it the Green Man?

Pause.

Was it the devil?

Jethro Let's go home.

SCENE THREE

The Duke of York's palace. Marion, daughter of the Duke of York, in a furious argument with Makepeace, her guardian.

Makepeace You will marry Geoffrey of Shrewsbury.

Marion Geoffrey of Shewsbury is an asparagus.

Makepeace A wealthy and connected young man . . .

Marion Lacking only a brain and two legs of similar length.

Makepeace You choose to defy me?

Marion My father has not given you the power to decide my future husband. He will return from the crusade and he will decide who I marry.

Makepeace You are already sixteen years old. Your father could be away for years longer fighting the infidel. Who will have you then?

Marion Then I shall die a maid.

Makepeace And what if, God forbid, your father dies? On the field of battle? Your mother already in heaven?

Marion You have no need to remind me.

Makepeace Then officially, as your guardian, I, Arthur Makepeace, will own you. I will do what I like with you.

Pause. A threat.

Marion My father will not die. He will return within the month.

Makepeace How do you know that?

Marion I have it in his own hand in this letter.

Makepeace Show me.

Marion It is not for your eyes.

Makepeace I will make known to Geoffrey your decision.

He leaves. Marion buries herself in her letter. Her sister Alice enters.

Alice What are you reading, sister?

Marion Nothing.

Alice If it is nothing, then there is nothing to hide. (*Looks closer.*) You are crying!

Marion Not at all. An Aquitainean onion came close to my eye, that's all.

Alice Let me see.

Marion The letter is for me.

Alice Let me see!

Alice grabs the letter. Reads.

Marion Don't read it.

Alice Oh look. It's from Father!

Marion Don't read it, Alice.

Alice 'Dearest daughter Marion. Our crusade is delayed here at Acre. Months doing nothing, our king angrier by the day. I shall not be back this next year. Be warned. In his absence, King Richard has given fiefdom of our lands to his brother John. John will soon make a visit to York with his men.'

Oh how exciting! The King's brother coming to our castle. I've heard he's terribly handsome.

Marion John? He is as ugly as a frog.

Alice He will flirt with us, of course. Gaze longingly into our eyes.

Marion If he can find a stool to stand on.

Alice There's more. (*She reads.*) 'Marion, do look after your sister. You know how her empty brain can be turned by power and money.'

Pause.

Daddy's just being funny. I need a new dress. Lace trimming in the corsage. French style.

Marion Sister, did you not read? Father will not be back for a year!

Alice Oh, you're missing him. Me too.

Marion Without Father, this house has no life. For two years it has been filled with pretenders to his position, lickspittles, fawners and flatterers. And now the greatest pretender of them all, John, is set to sully our walls.

Alice Marion. That is treason. Prince John may one day be king of this country.

Marion Then truth will finally have fled its shores. We live in the age of shallowness.

Alice Marion, stop it.

Marion All purity shed in the landgrab. Kingdoms sold for a song, forests stolen and turned into game parks, entertainment for the chattering classes . . .

Alice Is that the time? I must say my prayers and then the lute.

She leaves. Marion continues. To herself. To us.

Marion All principle and integrity sacrificed on the altar of preferment. Only my father stood strong against the raging torrent of ambition. He refused false favours, took no bribes, made no deals. Now he fights for his country in some faraway war that seems to make less and less sense to him. And I am left here on the ramparts of a castle whose stones can only stare and weep. Will he ever return?

Pierre enters, hair like a meringue.

Pierre Ah, the uplifting tones of my mistress. I have been asked to enquire whether you would prefer the salmon or the whiting for lunch –

She throws something at him.

– whether you prefer dahlias or mild thyme in the courtyard garden –

And something else.

– and whether you will consider marrying Geoffrey of Shrewsbury.

Marion AAAAAGH! Take this stick. Fight me.

Pierre Madam, I am no fighter. As you know.

Marion Fight me!

Pierre Should you desire a chanson, or a silly jig . . .

Marion Stand and fight.

Pierre Madam, I really . . . Ow! That hurt.

Marion Come on then! Fight!

Pierre Fight a mere girl? Never. Ow! Right, that's it.

*He tries to fight her, but he is rubbish and she is
brilliant. She beats him, pinions him to the ground.*

Marion If you were John, brother of the King, I would
take this stick to your neck and with one slice . . .

She makes to behead him.

Pierre I'm not him. I'm your talented, slightly overweight,
peace-loving servant Pierre.

Marion I will die in this castle!

Pierre This'll cheer you up. Did you hear what happened
to Thomas LeBrun? He was riding through Sherwood
forest on his way here to deliver your letter. And who
should stop him in the forest but a certain Robin Hood.

Marion I thought he was dead.

Pierre Apparently not. LeBrun and spouse were by all
accounts stripped of their clothes and gold and made to
pull their own carriage all the way to York. Ha ha ha!

Marion But of course. (*Beat.*) That's it.

Pierre What is?

Marion Pack me a suitcase. One change of clothes.

Pierre Where are you going?

Marion Into the forest.

Pierre Explain.

Marion My father will not return for a year or more. Until he does I can no longer stay in this corrupted castle. I will join Robin Hood and his men.

Pierre Are you mad? He's a ruffian. A criminal.

Marion I hear he steals only from the rich.

Pierre Romantic nonsense. He steals from anyone who's stupid enough to come across him.

Marion Well, we are about to find out. Tonight, after sundown, we will take the back path out of the kitchens and flee into the forest.

Pierre Hold on . . .

Marion We will meet this noble savage . . . and we will question him . . .

Pierre Just a minute.

Marion If he is, as I suspect him to be, a good man with a heart brave and true, we will join his merry men and until my father returns we will not step one foot into this godforsaken . . .

Pierre WE?!

Marion Well, of course you're coming with me.

Pierre Do I strike you as the forest type?

She looks at him.

Marion You'll need to do something with your hair. Meet me outside the charnel house at midnight.

Pierre I refuse!

Marion Imagine, sleeping under the stars, waking with the deer, swimming in rivers, and setting wrongs to right.

Pierre I'm telling your guardian. This is the deranged workings of an under-employed female imagination.

Marion Brave, faithful Pierre.

She kisses him.

Pierre I'll regret this.

Marion The good man never regrets.

SCENE FOUR

Thunder in the forest. Robin and his men usher in a Friar in cloak and gown, tied up in a rope.

Robin Bring him to our camp.

Friar In touching me you offend God himself! Hear how he rages at your villainy!

More thunder.

Much Give us the money you have, we'll have no need to touch you.

Friar I have nothing. I am a holy man, travelling through the land seeking shelter and alms as I go. Touch me and I will bring the wrath of God down upon you with all its might! He will lacerate your skin with boils, chill your pagan blood . . .

Little John I know you. I have seen you at market selling false rosary beads.

Friar That is a lie!

Little John And using your own urine as holy water.

Friar In impugning me you impugn the word of God.

Robin I want to hear the word of God. Climb that tree and tell us of our sins.

Friar What – now? In this weather?

Robin Will God not protect your holiness?

He climbs. Lightning flashes.

Friar *Et retribuit mihi Dominus secundum iustitiam meam . . .*

Robin In common English. For we are common men.

Friar It is a sin to speak God's word in common tongue.

Robin Then it should be a common sin. In English.

Friar And the Lord will reward me according to my justice; and will repay me according to the cleanness of my hands:
Because I have kept the ways of the Lord; and have not done wickedly against my God.
And I shall be spotless with him: and shall keep myself from my iniquity!

Robin shakes the tree.

What are you doing?

Robin Keep talking.

Friar For thou wilt save the humble people; but wilt bring down the eyes of the –

Robin shakes the tree. A coin falls from beneath the Friar's cloak. Then more. Then a fountain.

Robin Pennies from heaven.

They rush to pick up the coins. A voice from offstage.

Marion Robin Hood! Where are you? We are full of riches!

Will Who is that?

Much The voice of an angel!

Little John A wealthy angel.

Marion We are lined in silver and gold!

Robin In the trees.

They hide. Marion enters with Pierre.

Marion We are weighed down by booty!

Pierre With despair, more like. Can we please go home?

Marion Why isn't anyone coming? What does it take for a duke's daughter to be robbed these days?

A lightning flash. They see the Friar in the tree. Pierre throws himself on the ground.

Pierre Forgive me, Father, for I have sinned. I stole some bread from Marion's plate at lunch and I lusted after Mary the goatherd's daughter, she with the ankles of carved willow and the softest . . .

Marion kicks Pierre.

Marion My name is Marion, daughter of the Duke of York. I seek the man they call Hood. Robin Hood.

Friar Begone, sweet mistress.

Marion Why?

Friar Evil stands close by. Take flight from the devil's horseman!

Pierre (*to Marion, terrified*) I want to go home!

Marion (*to Friar*) If you know where Robin Hood is, then tell him I am not afraid of him! Tell him that Marion, daughter of the Duke of York wishes to . . .

Enter Will, John, Much.

Wishes to . . .

Enter Robin.

Robin Wishes to what?

Pierre To go back to her nice cosy castle . . .

Marion Wishes to join you!

Pause.

I wish to join you and your merry men.

Robin There's nothing merry about us, mistress. Best be on your way.

Marion I am staying here.

Robin Best be home.

Little John Did you hear him, princess?

Pierre Keep away from her!

Little John Says who?

Little John fronts up to Pierre.

Pierre Ah! Get him away from me.

Marion (*to Robin*) Take everything. I shall require no comfort, no food nor lodging different to any of you rough men. I shall earn my share.

Pause. She removes her wealthy clothes.

These I divide amongst you as your equal.

Robin Did you not hear me? Take your clothes and go home.

Marion I HAVE NO HOME.

Pause. She cries.

I have no home. My father is far away and my castle is governed by monsters.

Will Poor girl seems in need, chief.

Much (*biting the gold jewellery*) Her gold is good.

Little John Her clown would make a good meal.

Robin No women in camp. Send her home.

Marion I won't go.

Robin Then you shall die at my hand, woman or no.

Marion You wouldn't touch me. A noblewoman, chaste, unarmed.

Robin Oh no?

> *Robin turns and with one blow, seems to be about to behead her. Instead he turns and beheads the Friar. Marion screams. Pierre holds her.*

This place is not for you.

Marion I thought you were a good man. That you stole from the rich only to give to the poor.

Robin You've been reading too many romances.

Marion But you're just a ruffian. A low-down, base . . . beggarly . . .

Robin Careful now.

Marion Come, Pierre. We don't belong here.

> *Marion leaves.*

Little John (*to Pierre, as he is leaving*) Yes, go on – run! Run! You globe!

> *Pierre leaves fast.*

Robin Bury the monk. Put his head on a stake and leave it at the edge of camp. I've had enough visitors for today.

SCENE FIVE

Marion and Pierre in the garden of the castle.

Marion How could he kill him without thought or conscience? A holy man.

Pierre I know that particular holy man. I think God may see it both ways.

Marion I thought Robin Hood was a moral outlaw. But he's just a thug.

Pierre Look, we're not far from the castle, no one will have missed us. We'll say we took a morning stroll to look at the lambs. If we hurry we can still make the main meal.

Marion Why were the castle walls made, Pierre?

Pierre To keep the enemy out.

Marion No. To keep me in. We are looking at my prison. I can't go back. I can't.

Enter Alice.

Alice There you are, Marion! Not weeping again! We've all been sent by our guest to look for you! And in this awful woodland and in these shoes.

Marion Guest?

Alice Have you not heard? The King's brother arrived this morning. What a man! Even the name blazes authority. JOHN! He has heard all about you, sister. And about me too, of course, but I am betrothed to dear Hubert of Leicester. John has heard talk of your beauty. That you have refused all suitors. He desires audience with you. And more than just audience . . . (*She laughs suggestively.*) I'm going to fetch him.

Marion No, Alice, don't.

Alice Don't be silly. He'll be so pleased.

Exit.

Marion Pierre, I am doomed. I cannot refuse the King's brother.

Pierre Well, you can. But you may end up in a frozen cell in some Norfolk castle left hanging by your ankles till you die of thirst.

Marion And I cannot go back into the forest.

Pierre Well, you can. But you may end up . . .

Marion Hide me.

Pierre Madam, this is not a child's game. John is the King's brother. He is of fierce temper –

Marion – and legendary sexual appetite.

Pause.

Help me, Pierre. Please.

Pierre Take my travelling sack.

Marion I can't hide in that.

Pierre Inside are my spare clothes from our ill-fated adventure into the forest. Go behind that hawthorn and put them on. Quick!

Marion hides. Enter Prince John, Makepeace and Guy of Gisborne.

John Taxes will need to double in all the towns. I am implementing a new levy on all households to support the crusades. It shall be called the Holy Contribution.

Makepeace These taxes will not prove popular with winter upon us.

John My brother is fighting a war against the Muslim terror. Do the people of this country wish to be overtaken by the hordes of Saladin? Raping our women? Burning our holy shrines? Then we require a full purse with which to fund our righteous campaign. Tell them that. If they still complain, Gisborne here will provide more forceful forms of argument.

He sees Pierre.

Who is this?

Pierre Good day, Your Majesty.

Pause.

John I am not king of this country . . .

Pierre No, of course . . . my error . . .

John Not yet.

Makepeace My liege, This is Marion's servant and buffoon.

John Where is she? Don't play games with me, clown.

Pierre My liege, I saw her early this morning on the other side of the castle watching the boys at the tiltyard. She did mention going on a very long walk over in that direction.

John strikes Pierre.

My liege, please may I ask why I deserved that?

John My future bride must never be left to walk alone in the forest.

He strikes Pierre again.

Pierre And that?

John I don't like clowns. They are thoroughly pointless.

Makepeace What are you doing here, Pierre?

Pierre Me . . . . I was just . . .

Marion We were looking for Marion.

Marion comes out from the bush dressed in Pierre's clothes.

Pierre Yes, we were looking for Marion. Been looking for hours, can't see her anywhere.

John Who is this?

Pierre This is my –

Marion – brother . . .

Pierre Brother.

Marion Martin.

Pierre Martin.

Marion My liege. I have heard talk of your many virtues.

John A fine figure of a man. Far more handsome than your brother.

Marion Thank you, my liege.

John You're not a clown, are you?

Marion I am a soldier, sir.

John Why are you not on crusade?

Marion Injured at Carthage, sir.

Pierre Hence the limp.

She limps.

Well, we must go and find that silly mare Marion.

John Wait. I wish to talk with your brother. I need new retinue. You should join me.

Marion I should very much like to, sir.

John Are you married, Martin?

Marion No, sir.

John But the ladies like you, don't they?

Marion Oh I don't know, sir. (*She laughs heartily.*)

John Oh I think they do. (*He laughs.*) The ladies like me too. (*He stops laughing.*) Eventually.

　He stares at her.

Tell me, what do you think of the Duke's daughter – Marion?

Marion Oh she's not much to speak of.

John That's not what I heard.

Marion She is thick-lipped, dark-eyed, stunted of growth, stale of scent and without a sharp wit in her head.

Makepeace How dare you, sir?!

John Ha ha! Let him be. I like this fellow. He would put me off sweet Marion as he has eyes for her himself. But I know her to be the finest maiden in all middle England. I will have her to wife. And the more spirit she has, the more I shall enjoy bringing it to heel. Women are like horses in that respect.

Marion It's all in the breaking in.

John So rare to find a man who truly understands me. Makepeace, I want that girl brought to me by lunch or I shall remove you as guardian of this castle.

　Exit.

Makepeace Find her. Both of you. Your lives depend on it.

Exit. Marion kisses Pierre passionately.

Pierre Was that for saving your life? Or just sheer unbridled desire . . .

Marion It was for giving me an idea. Come on.

Pierre Where are we going?

Marion Back into the forest.

Pierre Mistress –

Marion Not mistress. Master. Master Martin of Sherwood.

Pierre What?

Marion I am going to form my own band of merry men. We will rob from the rich and give to the poor. I will show Robin Hood what makes a true noble outlaw. And you, dear brother Pierre, are coming with me.

Exit.

Pierre What have I done?

End of Act One.

Act Two

SCENE ONE

Castleton. The cottage. Jethro and Sarah. Rain pours down.

Sarah The house next door is boarded up.

Jethro That's seven houses in the town.

Enter their father, Robert Summers, ready for work with his dog Plug.

Father What are you two gossiping about?

Jethro Why is everyone leaving Castleton, Father?

Father People are foolish. It rains for ten days and they think the devil is coming.

Sarah Is he?

Father Of course not. There are no devils here.

Sarah Don't go to work today, Father.

Father You have your brother. He'll protect you.

She won't let go of him.

I'll leave the dog with you while I work, Sarah. There's no reason to fear.

He kisses them both and leaves. Pause. The rain falls. Wind howls. The dog comforts Sarah.

Jethro You're not scared, are you, Plug?

Plug shakes his head. The children laugh.

Chase me, Plug. Chase me!

Suddenly soldiers storm into the cottage, Gisborne at the helm. Plug growls.

Gisborne Where is your father?

Jethro In the fields.

Gisborne Mother?

Jethro In her grave. Two winters back.

Gisborne Your father has not paid the Holy Contribution. Tell him he has until sundown. Anyone on the list who has not paid by then will encounter the wrath of John, Earl of Nottingham, Lord of Sherbourne and Prince Regent of the Realm.

Sarah Why does he have so many names?

Pause.

Gisborne Sundown.

Jethro Father won't pay. He thinks it's wrong.

Gisborne What did you say?

Jethro Our mother died because she could not feed us. All our money goes to the Church and King. It's wrong.

Gisborne What's your name, boy?

Jethro Jethro Summers, sir. Son of Robert Summers and Rebecca Summers.

Gisborne How old are you?

Jethro Twelve, sir.

Gisborne Then you're old enough to understand. Your father will pay. One way or another. Tell him that.

SCENE TWO

The forest. Little John, Much, Will, Robin.

Little John Carriage coming.

The men hide. The carriage enters and the men swoop on it.

Robin Halt there. Come out of the carriage with your arms raised high.

A very fat Lord and Lady enter from the carriage. Already in their underwear.

What's this?

Lord We have already been robbed, sir.

Robin What do you mean?

Lord But an hour ago as we travelled through the northern stretch of forest a brigand and his gang swooped upon us and stripped us of everything.

Robin Search the carriage, Little John. Who robbed you?

Lady The most appalling devilish rogue, a fearful apparition. He calls himself . . .

Lord Martin of Sherwood.

Lady He has a sidekick. Big Peter. A terrifying creature with strange shoes.

Will That's three times this month they've beaten us to it.

Little John Carriage is empty, chief.

Lady Martin of Sherwood took it all.

Much There *is* no Martin of Sherwood! There is only Robin and his men. We are the outlaws of the forest and no one else.

Robin What is he like, this Martin of Sherwood?

Lady A mysterious figure. His voice is quiet and boyish. He behaves always with courtesy but quicker than thought he steals all your wealth.

Lord He has a kerchief over his chin and wears a green hat which he never takes off.

Lady He is almost frighteningly handsome. Pale skin. Eyes like gems. To be robbed by him was almost a privilege.

Robin He doesn't just rob them, he seduces them too.

Will Robin, he's getting in our business.

Little John This Martin needs to be taught a lesson.

Much He's taking what's ours by right.

Robin We need your carriage.

Lord But that's all we have left!

Robin You have your legs. Use them. Unless you want me to take those as well.

Lord and Lady leave.

Paint the carriage red. It's time to pay Martin of Sherwood a visit.

SCENE THREE

The castle at York. John at feast. Huge tables of food. Alice. Makepeace.

John I have to have her!

Makepeace I have men scouring the forest. But it has been several weeks now. I fear she has either been taken by outlaws or eaten by animals.

John And I never even saw her.

Alice She looked a little like me. But more pinched.

John Are you sad to lose your sister?

Alice Terribly. Grief is now my only sibling. (*She sniffles.*)

John I was going to marry her, you know. Every report told me of her beauty.

Alice My Lord Regent. As you know, I am betrothed to Hubert of Leicester.

John No, I didn't.

Alice Dear sweet Hubert. My only angel. But if, for the sake of the kingdom, and the preservation of your royal honour . . . I should need to forsake Hubert, dear sweet Hubert, for a greater man –

John What are you saying?

Alice I am willing to serve you utterly. And totally.

John But I don't want you. You are old and vain. I want *her*. God intends her beauty for me.

    Pause.

Hubert is not yet knighted, is he?

Alice He is as yet merely plain Hubert. He would be Sir Hubert but for the fact that he was not able to join the crusade due to an unfortunate fear of spiders which as you know much prevail in the Levant.

John I will knight him –

Alice Oh, my lord.

John – if you find your sister. I think she fled the castle to escape me.

Alice Surely not. How could she?

John She is honest. That excites me. She is spirited. That thrills me. Take some men to protect you. Go out each day until you find her, and persuade her to return.

Alice You mean . . . go into the forest . . . me?

John And Hubert will have his knighthood, a castle and a dominion all to his own.

Alice I live only to serve.

Exit.

John I want grouse.

Enter Gisborne.

Gisborne We have collected the Holy Contribution from Castleton, York and Dewsbury.

John Any resistance?

Gisborne In York and Dewsbury, some peasant muttering but nothing serious. In Castleton, however . . .

John What?

Gisborne Three men are refusing to pay. Samuel Tyler, Randall Kerrick and Robert Summers.

Makepeace They claim that it is not lawful for the Regent to feast while his subjects starve.

John The Holy Contribution is for the war campaign.

Makepeace They claim that the money is not reaching the war effort.

John How dare they?! That is God's gold. Arrest them. Charge them with treason and apostasy. Do they have families?

Makepeace The first two are younger men. Robert Summers is a widower. He has a son and daughter.

John Charge them all.

Makepeace Including the children?

John Children need to learn their lessons, don't they?

Marion dressed as Martin and Pierre dressed as Big Peter are eating lamb chops. They have donned outlaw clothes of the greensward.

Marion Isn't this the life, Peter? Roasting lamb on an open fire, lamb that we caught ourselves, killed ourselves, bled and gutted . . . What's wrong?

Peter I'm not hungry. And my name is not Peter. It's Pierre. It's French, Gallic, stylish.

Marion It's Peter. Big Peter.

Pierre Shut up.

Marion How dare you?

Pierre You're not a duke's daughter any more, I can call you what I like. You have taken me from the warmth of my toasty bed with its crumpled linen and my little bear Bramble –

Marion Not him again.

Pierre – and exposed me to the fretful elements with no care for my well-being. You know how much I hate the country. I have cold bones. And green isn't my colour.

 Enter a poor Peasant.

Peasant I seek alms.

Marion (*changing her voice*) Ah, you poor suffering man. Come with me.

Pierre Here we go.

Marion There's gold for you.

Peasant Thank you, sir.

33

Marion Tell your kin that any poor man or woman that comes will be given gold equally. For Martin of Sherwood is a noble outlaw.

Exit Peasant.

Pierre He's been three times this week.

Marion Nonsense.

Pierre All this goodness can get very irritating, you know.

Marion How can you say that? We have robbed six carriages. We have taken jewels and gold.

Pierre And then given it away to the poor!

Marion What greater thrill? To take from those that only receive and give to those who do nothing but grieve. We'll show Robin Hood what it is to be a true man of the forest.

Pierre You strike me as rather obsessed by him.

Marion Nonsense.

Pierre All you do is talk about him. Robin Robin Robin. I'm just saying.

Marion Well, don't. Listen to the birds. We are free as them. Oh Pierre. Have you ever felt such joy?

Pause. The sound of a carriage.

Pierre That's not birds.

Marion That's singing. And that's the carriage of a rich man. Peter, come on. Into the trees!

Pierre I've just eaten.

Marion Get up!

Pause. Enter a carriage. Accompanied by rich men apparently singing inside. The carriage painted red.

34

Song
> Oh the life of a rich man
> Is better than life in a ditch man
> For rough clothes can make your skin itch man
> But never the silk of the rich man!
> Of the rich man
> For we live the life of the rich man!

Marion swoops on the carriage and stops it.

Marion Halt there in the name of justice. Come out with your hands held high. No one need be harmed. Martin of Sherwood seeks only that earthly wealth which must die with you before your Lord.

Pause.

Come out.

She and Pierre approach the carriage.

Pierre Something's not right. The carriage. I recognise it. Two days ago.

Marion That was white. This is blood red.

Pierre But the decoration. Too similar.

Marion You're such a yellow-belly.

She opens the carriage. Two dummies hang inside the carriage. Marion screams.

Robin Martin of Sherwood, I presume.

Marion and Pierre are surrounded by Robin and his men. Marion screams lower.

And you must be Big Peter.

Pause.

Pierre That's me.

Little John He looks familiar.

Pierre Me? I've never met you before in my life!

Robin approaches Marion aggressively.

Robin Do you know what forest this is?

Marion This is Sherwood Forest.

Robin This is my forest.

Marion A forest is owned by no man.

Robin Not true. King and lords make forest laws to stake their claim over oak and deer. Now I have staked mine. This is my land. And you're on it.

Marion You steal only for yourself. I give everything I have to the poor. I am the just outlaw. You are a common thief.

Robin Where is your stash?

Marion I will not tell you.

Much Where?

Marion Kill me, but I will not tell you.

Robin You are a brave lad, Martin. Now, your friend here –

Marion – is also incorruptible.

Robin You use fine words for an outlaw. (*To Pierre.*) And is it true? Are you incorruptible?

Pierre Absolutely.

Robin What fine fingers you have. Long, slender.

Pierre They're from my mother. She's a seamstress, an enchantress of wool.

Robin Let me see.

Robin takes his hand. Raises his sword.

Pierre The stash is behind the oak, in a shallow pit.

Much and Will go.

Marion You coward!

Pierre Sorry.

Much and Will return.

Much There's a treasury in here.

Robin Take everything. And take their clothes too.

Marion No! Never!

Robin I said take them off.

Marion I will kill you first.

Robin You'll fight me, boy?

Marion On the branch across the river. The first to fall loses.

Robin If I win, you give me all your clothes. Every stitch.

Marion And if I win?

Robin You keep your gold.

Marion Let's fight.

They run to the river. A branch crosses it.

Pierre But mist— master!

Robin Swords or staffs?

Marion Swords.

The branch across the river. They fight. Robin wins.

Robin Your clothes, sir. All of them.

Pierre Oh dear.

Marion Let's fight again.

Robin What do I gain if I win this time?

Marion My life.

Pierre Mari— Martin! Think what you are doing!

Robin Your life?

Marion Or are you too much coward?

*They fight. A fantastic fight, both with great skill.
But . . . Robin wins.*

Robin You are truly brave, Martin. Kneel and I will
make your death fast.

She kneels.

Pierre My lord, stop. This man, this delicate, lovely,
effeminate, girlish man is not worthy of death. He is
young, foolish yes, reckless yes, but he is not dishonest.
His soul is as fair as his eye. Forgive him. Kill me instead.

He offers up his neck.

Marion Oh, Peter.

Pierre This forest's made me mad.

Enter a Townsman, fast.

Townsman Where is Martin of Sherwood?

Robin He is here, not long for this earth.

Townsman Martin of Sherwood, the town of Castleton
seeks your aid.

He falls to his knees.

The King's brother has brought in new taxes, causing
hunger and illness. Three men have refused to pay. Two
have already been executed in the town square. The
third, Robert Summers, has been taken to the castle by

Guy of Gisborne. Unless he recants he will die tonight.
And . . . oh Martin, you who are fair and good, his
family will die too.

Robin His family?

Townsman Two children. They too will taste the noose.
It is the Regent's royal command.

Pause.

I do not know you, sir.

Robin I am Robin Hood.

Beat.

Why do you flinch?

Townsman Your story runs before you like blood.

Robin Why seek you this wretch? What can he do to
save you?

Townsman He has helped many before. What he steals
he shares with the poor, and at this time he is all that
stands between us and starvation.

Much We steal.

Townsman Only for yourselves.

Little John It's a fair point.

Marion The family are all in the castle?

Townsman Execution is at dawn.

Will Then we only have tonight.

Robin No way into that castle.

Marion I know a way.

Robin Quiet, dead man.

Marion But I do!

Robin How? How do you know?

Pause.

Townsman Please, we have so little time.

Little John Sir! I humbly submit a request. If he does know a way in to the castle, suspend execution of Martin. Until tomorrow.

Will I second his request. Suspend execution.

Much I agree. There's a poor family might die tonight. We can't stand by.

Robin Why are you all so sudden to leap to arms? What do we gain from it?

Little John Two little ones, Robin. Die without us they will.

Robin Do you not remember our vow? We stand apart from the world of men. We look only to ourselves, owing no one, bound to no creed, with no weight on our souls.

Marion How can you say that when children are dying?

She beats at Robin's chest.

Robin What are you doing?

Marion Have you no heart at all inside that shell?

Pause.

Robin We will save this family. And tomorrow I slit your throat. You accept my conditions?

Marion I accept.

Robin Lead the way.

End of Act Two.

Act Three

SCENE ONE

The castle. A cell. Jethro and Sarah and their dog.
Makepeace with them.

Makepeace If your father submits to pay the Holy
Contribution, and to publicly repent his insubordination,
you will be free to leave.

Jethro And if he does not?

Makepeace Then . . .

Pause.

I will return shortly. Pray for your father, children.

He leaves.

Sarah Jethro, I don't like it here.

Jethro It will be all right. You know Father. He always
finds a way.

Sarah Tell me a story.

Jethro There was once a forest. And in the forest was a
giant. And the giant terrified all the animals, until one
day a brave girl called Sarah got lost in the forest with
her brother –

Sarah Jethro.

Jethro – Jethro, and their dog Plug. And they came upon
the giant's lair which was as high as a tree and as wide as
a lake. And they knocked at the door. And the giant
turned and in one swoop he leapt and grabbed his axe.

A sound of a gibbet's trapdoor.

Sarah Was that the giant?

Gisborne enters.

Gisborne Come with me.

Jethro Where are you taking us?

Gisborne Bring them.

Soldiers enter, grab the children and take them away.

SCENE TWO

John sits at a table. Gisborne is there. Soldiers. The hanging body of Robert Summers, Jethro and Sarah's father.

Alice bursts in.

Alice Every day I search for that wretched sister in that awful forest! Please don't make me do it any more! It's torture! It's a living death!

Am I interrupting?

She sees the body.

Oh, a body. How thrilling. Sorry, don't mind me.

John Bring them in.

A door opens. Jethro, Sarah and Plug are brought in. Sarah cries.

Jethro Summers. Define 'example'.

Jethro Sir?

John 'Example'. From the French – *exemple*. What does it mean?

Jethro It means one kind of a thing.

John Stop her crying! (*Sarah is muffled.*) Use the word in a sentence.

42

Jethro One example of an animal is a cow.

John Very good. Now my turn. I have just executed your father. I will tell you why I have done this. There are towns and villages all over this miserable freezing country filled with stubborn hard-headed fools just like him. I need their money. In punishing your father, I am educating them. I am setting an example. How old is your sister?

Jethro Eight.

John Would you like her to live to see nine?

Jethro Yes.

John Would *you* like to live, Jethro?

Jethro Yes.

John Bring in the paper.

An officer brings in a paper.

I would like you to read this in the town square tomorrow.

Jethro Can't read.

John Then you can memorise it. (*He reads.*) 'I, Jethro Summers, and my sister Sarah pledge allegiance to King Richard and his loyal brother John. I renounce my father Robert as a subversive, a dangerous rebel, an unbeliever, who turned from God to the devil and from the holy crown to the mouth of hell. I vow to obey Prince John in all his requests and to serve him as a new God-given father.'

Jethro I will never say that.

Makepeace Think, Jethro. Don't be hot-headed like your father.

Jethro My father is no traitor. He fought for the King against France. He loves his country. He loves it more than you do.

John Bring in the executioner. You godless villain!

Alice Kill him. Kill them both!

An executioner enters. Hooded. Terrifying.

Jethro Kill me. Spare her.

John Kill the girl first. He can watch.

Sarah is grabbed and a bag placed on her head. She is taken up to the gibbet.

Jethro Stop!

Pause.

'I, Jethro Summers, and my sister Sarah pledge allegiance to King Richard and his loyal brother John. I renounce my father Robert as a subversive, a dangerous rebel, an unbeliever, a heretic who turned from God to the devil and from the holy crown to the mouth of hell. I vow to obey the King's brother in all his requests and to serve him as a new . . . God-given . . . father.'

John Good boy. Executioner, you may leave us.

Robin But my liege, I've only just got here.

Robin takes the executioner's black mask off. The other outlaws swing in from the windows. Marion dressed as Martin.

John Soldiers!

A fight. Robin, Marion and their men against eight soldiers. In the fight Marion saves Robin's life. Marion takes Jethro and Robin takes Sarah and together they escape from the castle.

Who are you?

Robin Robin Hood.

Marion And Martin of Sherwood.

Robin Outlaws!

A battlefield in Europe.

Duke of York My dearest Marion. News has reached us on our crusade that Prince John is planning an uprising against his brother. I am returning with a power to England as fast as our horse will carry us. Do everything in your power to delay John's rebellion. I am relying on you, Marion. I know that you alone have the courage to stop him. Sealed with tears of grief and hope. Your loving father.

SCENE FOUR

The forest, by the oak. Sarah alone. Not speaking. Jethro trying to play with her. Plug also. Pierre and Marion.

Pierre Still the girl does not speak. She has said not one word since her father died.

Marion Jethro.

Jethro Yes, sir?

Marion Say something to your sister.

Jethro Sarah? Come and talk to the gentleman who rescued us. Sarah? Come and talk to Plug.

Silence. Marion holds the girl. Enter Robin and his men. Marion lets go, looks manly.

Robin Get some rest. Tomorrow we must conceal ourselves further within the forest.

Marion And in the morning? Am I still to die?

Pause. Everyone stares at Robin.

Robin I'm not a man to go back on my word.

Marion But?

Robin Seeing as you led us into the castle . . .

Marion And saved your life . . .

Robin If I let you live, do you agree to be under my command?

Marion No. Do you agree to be under mine?

Pause.

Robin I will spare you for now.

Marion Then we'll continue to work together.

Robin Until I can no longer stand you.

Marion Or I you.

Robin Then you shall die.

Marion Or you shall.

Robin You want to fight again?

Marion Ever eager.

Robin By the river?

Marion Bring it on!

Pierre Let's just all go to bed, shall we?

Pause.

Will Play some sleepy music, Much.

Pause. They rest and sleep. Much plays a song. Robin sits alone. Marion sees Robin. Approaches.

Marion You're not sleeping.

Robin Not you again.

Marion Don't you ever sleep?

Robin Just go to bed, Martin.

Marion I love the night. Night is when a forest sings.

Robin Night is when I can be on my own.

Pause.

Marion Why do you allow no women in your camp?

Robin How do you know that?

Marion One of your men . . . told me.

Robin Women cause tempests in the heart of man. They make us rash and unreliable.

Marion Have you never met a woman who was different to that?

Robin Never.

Pause.

Marion Have you never loved then?

Robin Never. (*Beat.*) Have you?

Marion Have I loved a woman?

Robin What else? A deer?

Marion No. Not a woman.

Robin You're young. Bet you barely kissed a girl.

Marion Barely have. (*Beat.*) But if I was to love . . . a woman –

Robin Yes?

Marion – she would be brave, impetuous, but still with a feminine grace.

Robin And a good body on her. (*He laughs.*)

Marion Yes, of course. (*She laughs.*)

Pause.

Robin I did meet one lass.

Marion Oh yes?

Robin It was nothing.

Marion No, go on! I mean if you want . . . I won't say a thing.

Robin Man to man?

Marion Man to man.

Robin It was here in the forest. Few weeks back.

Marion What was she like?

Robin She had something.

Marion What? What did she have?

Robin It wasn't her beauty. I've seen prettier women . . .

Marion Have you?

Robin But there was something . . . in her eyes . . . like when you looked her in the eye, she'd look straight back, like you are now . . . just . . .

Marion Right back at you.

Pause.

Robin Anyway, she was out of my league. Aristocracy.

Marion But what if what she was seeking was something beyond what she knew. Something dark and unfathomable.

They are close now.

Robin Well, she's gone now. Probably dead.

Marion How do you know?

Robin Type like that. Couldn't survive three nights in this forest.

Robin sleeps. Marion stays awake. She speaks to us and Plug.

Marion What do I do, Plug? I love him. He's brutish, he's emotionally unavailable, but I love him. How can I tell him my true feelings? How can I tell him who I am?

She takes off her hat. Unknown to her, Sarah is awake and looking at her.

If he knows that I am Marion he will send me away. I shall have to go back to the castle, or be eaten by wild animals. I am not sure which is the worse fate. Oh, not to be Marion!

She turns, sees Sarah staring at her. Puts her hat back on. Pause.

(*As Martin.*) Time for bed.

SCENE FIVE

Prince John and Makepeace.

Makepeace They are merely children, sir.

John Do you understand nothing? If word should spread, as spread it will, like boils, like plague, that I allowed tax evaders to survive, to laugh in my face, then my levies across the country will be ignored and dishonoured. I need that money.

Makepeace For the crusade.

John Yes, for the crusade.

Pause.

Makepeace I received this letter today. It was for Marion, from her father.

He hands it over.

The Holy Contribution is a lie. You are raising money to fund an army of your own. Against your brother Richard.

Pause.

John Yes, I am.

Makepeace Against the King?

John Yes, against the King. When Richard tries to return, I will have twenty thousand men, fully armed, across the south coast of England, ready to repel him. I already have the loyalty of London. I will seize the throne and England will have a new king. King John.

Makepeace That is treason!

Pause.

John How dare you?

Makepeace The Duke of York, the man I serve, is as loyal to the King as I am! You are a traitor, sir! Soldiers!

None come.

Soldiers!

Enter Gisborne.

John It would appear your power is on the wane, Makepeace. Best get back on the winning side.

Makepeace My lord, I entreat you – return to the godly path! Abandon this madness!

John Are you refusing to obey my command? Gisborne!

Gisborne My lord.

John Sir Arthur Makepeace needs to make a decision over where his true loyalty lies. Would you help him make it?

Makepeace Please, my lord . . . I beg you . . .

Gisborne seizes Makepeace.

John The problem with that tongue of yours, Makepeace, is that it wants to please everyone. It needs to learn that we can't all be happy all the time.

Gisborne grabs the tongue, takes a knife out, and with a slash cuts the tongue out.
He holds the tongue. Gives it to John.

Gisborne, go to the local farms, kill thirty pigs, bleed them, and collect the blood. Then get the keys to all the shrines of the town. Bring them to me.

Gisborne Sir.

John And Gisborne. Give this to my dogs. (*The tongue.*) Such a shame to waste such a well-exercised muscle.

SCENE SIX

Inside Castleton's chapel. Sunday. Villagers are entering to pray. Suddenly a woman cries out.

Villager Blood! Blood on the saint!

And now we see blood pouring from the mouth of the saint. Pouring out on to the chapel.

Villager 2 The other shrines are also bleeding!

Villager 3 We are damned! The devil is amongst us!

Panic in the chapel.
Castleton town square. A ranting Priest is speaking.

Priest There is a creeping evil in this town. When Robert Summers was killed we found that his tongue was forked and his eyes were full of blood. He had the devil inside him. He killed his wife and he lay with the devil's whore and his children are the spawn of the devil!

Townsman His children must be killed!

Priest And those that harbour them!

Townswoman And those that harbour them!

Townsmen Into the forest! Find Jethro and Sarah Summers! Kill them! Kill! Kill! Kill!

Flames are lit and the Townspeople head out of the town and into the forest. Behind, the Priest is met by Guy of Gisborne who hands him several pieces of gold.

SCENE SEVEN

The forest. Alice is with several soldiers.

Alice For weeks I've searched this miserable wood, and no sign of my sister. I so want to give her up for dead. Vicious little bitch. But then on the other hand to be Lady Alice of Leicester! What would I give for that? (*To her soldiers.*) Well, at least I have you.

Suddenly her soldiers fall, killed by arrows. Alice stops dead. Enter Much, Will, Robin, John.

Robin Mistake, lady, to walk unprotected in these parts.

Alice Do not touch me. I am the daughter of the Duke of York.

Robin Another one?

Much What is it with posh frocks and forests?

Alice You have met my sister Marion?

Robin May have done.

Alice Where is she? I must find her.

Will She wanted to join our merry men.

Alice Why doesn't that surprise me?

Robin Do you want to join?

Alice Join you? You filthy animal.

Robin Martin, see what we have found.

*Enter Marion, in disguise as Martin, with Pierre,
Jethro and Lucy. Marion stares in shock at her sister.*

Marion What are you doing here? (*Changes voice.*)
Lady.

Alice I am looking for my sister on behalf of Prince
John. He seeks her hand in marriage. I have already told
this ruffian that any harm that is done to me will be
punished by the Prince in the severest manner.

Marion Your sister isn't here. Now go home.

Alice Not until I find her. She has a duty to marry the
Regent to the realm.

Marion If she is as wilful as you describe . . .

Alice Stubborn more like. A mule.

Marion Then she will refuse your offer.

Alice It's not an offer. She will marry him or I will
personally throttle her.

Marion I'd like to see you try.

Pierre Sir . . .

Alice And what's it got to do with you, commoner?

Marion More than you might think, Lady Vanity.

Alice How dare you speak to me like that? I'll have you whipped to an inch of your life!

Marion I'll whip you myself!

Alice Just you try!

Jethro I can smell smoke.

Pause. Robin listens.

Robin Fire in the forest.

Enter Little John.

Little John Chief! The whole town are coming, with pitchforks high and branches flaming.

Robin What do they want?

Little John does not want to say.

Go on, man!

Little John They're after the little ones. They say they're the devil's children. They're saying . . . they want them killed.

Jethro hugs Sarah.

Robin How far away?

Little John Less than a mile. And circling in. No way out.

Marion On whose orders do they come?

Little John He who has the same name as me, but nothing else in common. The Prince.

Alice I told you he was not to be messed with. Oh, he'll kill you all. He'll take those two and throw them on the fire. He'll rip out your eyes and stand them on sticks so they can watch them burning! (*Out loud.*) They're this way! They are heading up to Barnett's Hill!

Robin Shut her up!

Much makes to kill her. Alice screams.

Marion NO!! I'll do it. You take the children. Hide them deep in the forest! I'll follow.

Robin Let's go!

They flee into the forest. Alice remains, terrified. The sound of the people approaching. Drumming. Smoke. Marion grabs Alice.

Alice Will you kill me?

Marion You know what? I should. Now go home and don't you dare so much as open your mouth to any soldier on your way.

Alice If we meet again, I'll show you my gratitude.

Marion Don't bother.

Alice runs.
The drumming intensifies. The smoke increases. Marion climbs a tree.

Hundreds of them. The forest is ablaze with flame. Jethro, Sarah! I'm coming!

Barnett's Hill. Robin and his men, Pierre, Jethro, Lucy. They are bringing in branches to make a camouflaged camp.

Jethro What will they do to us?

Robin Nothing. You're safe with us here. Come on!

Jethro My dad said you were a bad man.

Robin And what do you think?

Pause.

Look after your sister.

Jethro She won't speak.

Robin Sarah? It's going to be all right. Do you hear?

Silence. Enter Marion dressed as Martin. Pierre approaches her. Talks quietly.

Pierre (*aside to Marion*) You didn't actually kill her?

Marion (*aside to Pierre*) What do you think?

Robin Is she dead?

Marion (*out loud*) Put a blade through her heart.

Will They're coming up the hill. Flames everywhere.

Robin Hide under these branches.

They hide the children. John climbs the tree.

John They're coming closer. So many of them. The whole town.

Marion They will find them and they will kill them. There's no stopping it.

Robin They'll have to kill me first.

Much Kill all of us!

Marion Then they will kill you! We need another way!

Beat.

Peter. I know what I must do.

Pierre Are you sure?

Marion There's no other way.

Robin What?

Marion Wait for me here.

Robin Not another secret mission.

Marion Let me go. Please.

Pierre The only chance is if he goes alone.

Marion My leader. Give me your permission.

She goes on her knees. Pause. Robin nods.

Robin Do whatever you need. Just save these children.

Marion Give me as much time as you can.

She leaves. Will is still in the tree.

Will They're getting closer.

Robin We need to go higher. Children. Climb. Climb.

They climb the tree.
Elsewhere in the forest. Alice meets villagers with flames.

Alice The children are on Barnett's Hill! Find them and their protectors and kill them all!

Marion running through the forest. Dives down under leaves, avoids soldiers coming the other way. Runs on.
At the tree. Robin and the men and children climb higher. The townspeople surround the tree.

Townsmen Cut it down!

They start to cut down the tree.
In the castle. John and Gisborne. And Makepeace.

John Gisborne, when the deaths of the children are announced I want every city in the land to know. Use whatever method of rumour you can. Let it be clear how God punishes those who defy me.

Your thoughts, Makepeace?

Silence from the tongueless Makepeace.

I quite agree. We shall parade the children's bodies in the streets of the town. As for those who have protected them, round them up, pour boiling pitch into their mouths and hang them from the castle walls. I want to see them every morning when I head out for my ride.

Exit Gisborne.

You're regretting supporting me, aren't you, Makepeace? I ought to warn you, any attempt to escape will result in you losing a lot more than your tongue. I think we can still be friends. The sign of true friendship is what remains unspoken.

John leaves. Makepeace sits alone, weeping. Enter Marion dressed as Martin. Makepeace gets up, confused, tries to shout out, can't. Marion puts her hand over his mouth.

Marion Be quiet. Or I'll cut your tongue out.

Pause. Marion has a feel in Makepeace's mouth.

Oh, Makepeace, what have they done to you?!

She takes off her hat and kerchief. Makepeace tries to speak. He holds her, sobbing.

It is Marion. I have come to save the children's lives. Get me some of my own clothes from my chamber. Fast!

Makepeace rises and runs out. Gisborne enters. Marion replaces her hat and kerchief.

Gisborne Ah, the brother of the clown. We'd given up hope of you.

Marion Well, how wrong of you to do so. Would you please tell the Prince Regent that I have found the Duke's daughter Marion in the forest.

Gisborne Where is she?

Marion Close at hand. Bring the Prince to the banquet hall, I will present her to him.

In the trees. Robin and the children still climbing. The townsmen still cutting. Axe blows one by one.

Robin Climb, children. Climb.

Pierre Martin will come. I know he will!

Jethro Sarah, don't worry. He will come. He will come!

In the castle. Gisborne and John enter fast.

John Where is she?

Pause.

Where is the soldier?

Gisborne He was here, he said he had brought the girl back.

John If you've lost him again . . .

Enter Makepeace, who bows formally. And mimes an introduction.

Just get on with it! Where is my bride?

Enter Marion, stunningly dressed in a purple gown. Hair done. Cleaned up. Unrecognisable.

Marion I am here, my lord.

John moves to kiss her, consumed with lust.

John You are as they rumoured you to be. And so much more.

Marion And is the other rumour true also? That your desire is to marry me?

John It is.

Marion Then I am bound to accept with all earthly joy.

He makes to kiss her.

I have only one request in return. While away, I was taken by brigands.

John Robin Hood?

Marion The very same.

John He shall die.

Marion That is not my request. Among Hood's retinue are a girl and a boy. Young, innocent. Their lives are at risk. I want you to save them.

John It is not for a woman to involve herself with public affairs.

Marion kneels slowly.

Marion Grant this as a gift to the woman you love. I can marry anyone but I can give my heart only to a man I respect and adore.

John If I do this . . . will you give your heart to me without reserve?

Pause.

Marion I will.

She looks up at him.
In the trees. The tree falls. Robin and the children are left hanging from a branch of the next, then all fall.

Townsman Kill the children. Cut the devil out of them!

A fight. Robin, injured, fights valiantly, holding on to Sarah. But Jethro is grabbed and about to be cut open. Gisborne enters, shoots in the air.

Gisborne Wait!

He reads out a piece of paper.

'The Prince Regent John, Duke of Nottingham, Earl of Sherbourne, Duke of –'

Robin We know who he is!

Gisborne ' – forbids the murder of the two children. Although they have been possessed by the demons of hell, the Prince sends by royal order, this holy water, that when poured over them will drive out the devils and cure them.'

He ushers forward a Priest.

Pierre How did she do that?

Robin Who? Do what?

Pierre Nothing.

The water is poured over the children's heads. The Townsmen kneel.

Priest *Expelliamus demonem in nomine patris et filii et spiritus sancti.*

Townsmen *Expelliamus demonem in nomine patris et filii et spiritus sancti.*

The Priest casts out the devils, shaking as he does so.

Priest They are absolved and can return to the arms of Christ!

Townsmen Amen. Amen.

Robin I wish to take the children. They have no other parents.

Gisborne I am not ordered to prevent you.

Robin Come, Jethro. Come, Sarah. Come with us into the forest.

Robin and his men walk deep into the forest.

The castle. John and Marion.

John You make me want to be a good man, Marion. You have God in your eyes.

Marion I wish only to serve you.

John You will have that chance. We will marry very soon.

Marion When my father returns. It is a year, maybe a little more.

John Oh, dear sweet Marion. I can't wait that long. We will marry much sooner. Here are the banns.

Marion reads.

Marion 'The Lord Justice of the Realm announces the wedding of Prince John, Regent of the – (*She skips a bit.*) – to Marion, daughter to the Duke of York, at York Cathedral on 25th December in the year of Our Lord . . .' that's this year.

John Christmas Day. My idea.

Marion That's three days' time.

John What better day? Than the day of the birth of Our Lord?

He smiles at her.

Without reserve. Remember?

He kisses her at length and then leaves. Marion alone.

Marion ROBIN!!

End of Act Three.

Act Four

The forest. Dawn. Jethro and Sarah.

Jethro Christmas is coming, Sarah. We'll have Christmas in the forest. Maybe it will snow.

Pause.

Say something. You haven't said a word since we saw father hanging. He's in heaven now. Maybe he's one of those stars, smiling down. Can you see him?
Just one word, Sarah. One word.

Silence.

Let's go back to camp.

A wild boar appears.

Sarah, don't move.

Jethro grabs a branch, fights the wild boar as it tries to gore him. The boar attacks but Jethro parries, and forces it back. Pierre enters, sees the boar, screams and hides behind a rock. Then, as the boar attacks again, Jethro evades, turns to see Robin standing there. Robin throws him a fashioned spear and Jethro thrusts the spear into the boar's eye. The boar falls and dies.

Robin I do believe Jethro has caught our supper.

The boar is carried into camp. Music.

Pierre (*to us*) A week in the forest. God, meat tastes great when you've killed it yourself. What? I was there, wasn't I? Offering moral support? No, I'm getting into this life. Only one thing – a whole day and still no news from Marion. Where is she? What's happened to her?

Robin A toast to Jethro! For his first kill! Jethro – I anoint you a member of my merry men.

Will A toast to Martin! Wherever he may be. For saving the lives of our newest members.

Little John Where is Martin, chief?

Robin No word. I fear . . .

Little John You fear he is dead.

Robin It is possible he gave his life to save ours.

Will To Martin.

All To Martin!

They eat. Jethro approaches Robin.

Jethro Robin. Sarah still does not speak.

Robin One day she will. I know in my heart.

Jethro I don't think you're a bad man.

Enter Much.

Much News! News! So much news Much will make much brainwork deciding which to tell first.

Robin Try starting at the beginning and ending at the end.

Much But which is which? The news is that Martin was seen entering the castle just minutes before Prince John spared the children. A serving woman I met on the road . . .

Robin Met?

Much Met – robbed – and . . . But that's another story. She told me Martin has not been seen in the castle since he arrived!

64

Will He is imprisoned, Robin!

Much But the other news. Which is before during and after. The daughter of the Duke, Alice, the ugly two-faced harridan who nearly betrayed us, the one Martin said he killed. Is alive and back in the castle!

Robin Alive? But why would Martin lie?

Much And then the third piece of news. Stranger than the rest. Prince John is to marry the daughter of the Duke.

Robin Alice, the ugly two-faced harridan?

Much No – the one with fire in her eyes, and the unfunny clown.

Pierre leaps up, then sits straight down.

Robin Marion?

Much Yes, she who wanted to join our company. He is to marry her in two days!

Pierre leaps up, Robin also cries out.

Pierre / Robin NO!!

Pause.

Pierre Sorry. Nothing to do with me.

Robin Nor me.

Will What do we do, chief?

Pierre (*to us*) So here's my dilemma. Do I tell them who Martin is? But then the woman-hater Hood will turn his back on her – 'no women in camp'. But if I say nothing then they may do nothing to prevent this *affreux* marriage! (*Turns to Robin.*) I say we rescue Martin! He saved these children, the least we can do is honour him by trying to break into the castle.

Robin Big Peter is right. Our duty is to Martin! We must rescue him.

Much The castle dungeon is guarded by fifty men. There is no way in.

Robin My dear Much. There is always a way.

SCENE TWO

The castle. Marion is trying on a veil. Alice.

Alice Three days! A royal wedding! In York Minster! I must confess to disappointment that the Prince refused my request to marry Hubert on the same day. But I understand. This is your day, Marion, my dear. And I'm here to support you in whatever way you desire.

Marion You could go away.

Alice Your sense of humour. Delicious. I'm so pleased you got back safe. I was worried you would be eaten alive by wolves, your flesh ripped from your bones by talons and teeth. I even went to look for you myself. That's love. That's sisterhood.

Marion How did you get back?

Alice I met this outlaw. His name was Martin. Terrifying man. Huge. He wanted me, of course. Fell completely in love, as savages do when they meet a member of the higher class.

Marion But you resisted this Martin, did you?

Alice I'm pleased to say I did. But enough about me. How was your time in the wild?

Marion The happiest days of my life.

Alice laughs.

Alice Oh . . . . Delicious . . . you are . . . . Ha ha ha . . .

Enter John.

John Let me see my bride. My dear, I have come to take you to the priest for confession.

Alice Your soul will be as white as your wedding dress, sister. I'll get your coat.

She leaves. John hands Marion a letter.

John This letter came for you while you were away. It's from your father. Read it.

She reads it. Pause. Alice returns with the coat. Watches.

I show this to you as I feel we need to discuss where your allegiance lies. I have to trust you, Marion. When we are married we will travel the country together to enforce the Holy Contribution. I must be able to rely on you.

Marion The Holy Contribution is not for the crusades. It is for your own pockets to create an army to fight our king!

John That's right.

Marion I will never fight against my own king. And my own father.

John Marion, when you marry me, you cease to be obliged to your father. Your obligation rests entirely with me. YOU WILL OBEY ME. Is that clear?

Marion Never against my father!

He grabs a seamstress's needles, approaches her.

John A king's wife cannot refuse her master. Or she becomes a heretic. And Gisborne deals with heretics in the dungeons of Norfolk. Get your coat and join me in the carriage. The bishop awaits.

He leaves.

Marion Help me, Alice. Please.

Alice gives Marion the coat as if to help her put it on. Then twists her arm hard.

Alice How dare you cross your future husband? I am ashamed to call you sister.

She leaves. Marion weeps.

Marion Makepeace. Get me paper. I must get word to my father in France of what is happening here!

Makepeace writes something down. She reads it.

'He will allow no letters out of the castle.' Oh, this is torture!

Enter Gisborne.

Gisborne Come.

Gisborne escorts Marion. John stops him at the door.

John Gisborne. While we are at the cathedral, go out into the forest. Find the two children and kill them. Make it look like an accident. When you kill a man it's best remove his offspring too, lest they come back to haunt you.

Gisborne What shall I do with the bodies?

John Throw them down a well or something. I don't want my love to know anything about it. It would quite ruin the wedding.

SCENE THREE

York Minster. The Priest is offering confession.

Citizen Father, forgive me for I have sinned. I have stolen apples from my neighbour's gardens.

68

Priest *Misereatur tui omnipotens Deus, et dimissis peccatis tuis, perducat te ad vitam aeternam. Amen.*

Citizen Two Father, I have sinned. I have watched my neighbour's wife undressing at kiln-hole.

Priest As the Lord is merciful so he forgives you and grants you his infinite mercy and sends you forth pure of soul, be good in your actions as you have been honest in your confession.

Enter a third citizen. Actually Robin.

Robin Father, forgive me for I am about to sin.

Priest About to sin?

Robin Yes. I am about to take by force a religious man, steal his clothes and impersonate him for the furthering of my own interests.

Pause. The Priest tries to run. But Much, Will and Little John are outside.

Forgive us, Father. For what we know exactly what we do.

SCENE FOUR

Pierre, Jethro and Sarah. Plug there too.

Pierre So I'm the baby-sitter. They've gone to do lots of derring-do, saving Martin, breaking into castles. They don't even know who Martin really is! I do! I know! But what do I get? Big Peter? He gets to stay with the kids.

Sarah doesn't say a word.

I'm not sure she'll ever speak again. He just sits there whittling wood, and if I try to speak to him, he calls me a stuffed goose.

Jethro Get away from me, you stuffed goose.

Pierre You see, Plug? No thanks in this world. No gratitude from young to old, not like when I was a child.

Enter Gisborne. Pierre doesn't see him. Plug growls and hides in the trees.

I knew the meaning of respect. My father brought me up to believe in three things. Respect. Vigilance.

Jethro Peter . . .

Pierre Shhh, I'm talking. Respect. Vigilance . . .

Jethro But Peter . . .

Pierre I said shut it, shorty!

Pierre sees Gisborne.

Oh dear.

Gisborne I'm here for the children. Be wise. Don't get involved.

He holds his sword.

Pierre But what shall I tell the others?

Gisborne Say you were attacked by a wolf. An accident.

He cuts Peter on the arm.

Pierre Aaah!

Gisborne See. Claw scratch.

Pierre What will you do with them?

Gisborne That's not your concern. Come with me, children.

Jethro No.

Gisborne grabs Jethro, knife at his throat.

Gisborne Come.

He starts to move away with the kids.

Pierre Wait!

Gisborne turns.

You're not taking them. Not with me here. I am their protector.

Pause. Gisborne laughs.

Gisborne And who . . . are you?

Pierre I . . . am Big Peter.

Gisborne Are you now?

Gisborne attacks. Pierre defends himself with a branch. Reminder of the first scene when Marion fought him. But he is about to be killed when Plug dashes out of the bush and bites Gisborne. Gisborne roars. Jethro takes the stick he has been whittling and thrusts it between Gisborne's shoulders.

Pierre Run, children. Run!

They run into the forest. Gisborne pulls the stick out and roars in pain.

SCENE FIVE

York Minster. Smoke, incense. Singing. Censers. Marion and John. Guarded by soldiers.

John Your confessor is here. Listen to him and confess all your sins, for you must be pure as winter snow when you take my royal hand.

The Confessor enters. It is Robin Hood.

Welcome, confessor.

Robin *In nomine patris et filii et spiritus sancti. Amen.*

John Shrive the child.

Robin *Indulgentiam, absolutionem, et remissionem peccatorum tuorum tribuat tibi omnipotens et misericors Dominus. Amen.*

John And Bishop, if she says anything about her father, I want to know.

Robin A confession is a private matter between the penitent and their God.

John Not in my kingdom.

Robin nods. Marion still has not turned round.

Marion I will not say a word to you. I have nothing to confess but my own misery.

Robin Your debt now, child, is to your new husband to whom you must offer adoration, slavish love and complete physical surrender.

Marion I will do no such thing!

She turns. Robin is there. The censers are his merry men.

Robin of Sherwood.

Robin You remember me, princess? Our meeting was brief.

Marion Yes. I just about remember you.

Robin May I congratulate you on your marriage?

Marion You may not.

Robin Is the match not then a source of happiness to you?

Marion Why are you here? Not on my account?

Robin No, madam.

Marion No, of course. I am but a woman. Not worth the sweat of a man's labour.

Robin I am trying to rescue a comrade of mine. Martin of Sherwood. Do you know him?

Marion Martin of Sherwood?

Robin A brave man who saved the lives of two children in my care. We believe he was imprisoned in the castle for his pains. He may be being tortured as we speak.

Marion He is.

Robin You know where he is?

Marion I do. The pains he feels are beyond imagining. The lash. The barbed wire. The heavy cannon ball crushing his heart. These agonies are his daily bread.

Much We must save him!

Robin Please tell me where he is.

Pause.

Marion He is in the castle. Guarded day and night. He is never alone.

Robin So there is no chance of rescue?

Marion None. Unless . . .

Pause.

Find a way into the castle the night before the wedding. I will bring Martin out of the dungeons and into my chambers. Then you can take him with you and no one will know.

Robin I will do as you say.

Marion The night before the wedding, then.

Pause.

And Robin. I have a favour to ask in return.

Robin It is yours.

Marion Send secretly this letter to my father. It tells him everything of John's evil plans and urges his return.

She hands him a letter.

Robin You do not lack for courage, princess.

Will (*at the door*) The Prince returns! Put back your cowl!

Robin May I ask why your marriage affords you no joy?

Marion You may not.

Robin Perhaps you love another?

Marion Presume not to ask about my love. I am not of your party.

Will Robin, put back the cowl!

Robin A woman should never marry without love. For her heart will shrivel like a dried nut.

Marion What do you know of women? What do you know goes on inside a beating heart?

Little John Robin! This is no time for a chat!

Pause. Robin disguises himself.

Robin Together we will save Martin's life. That is all that matters.

Marion It is my deepest wish.

John returns with soldiers.

John Purified, my dear? Then let us return to the castle.

SCENE SIX

The forest. Pierre. Snow falling.

Pierre I've lost them! Gisborne hunted us down despite
his injury and in the chaos of flight I lost the children!
Damnation fall on my wretched head! I believe I love
them as they were my own. And now the snow is falling
and the winter cold will freeze their tiny bones.

A noise in the forest. He turns fast. It is Plug the dog.

Oh, great. Just who I need. A great help you're going to
be. And Robin has not returned and all is lost! Oh
Pierre! Pierre! Fool! Idiot! Coward!

But Plug suddenly goes on hind legs, smelling something.

What is it? (*He listens.*) You can smell something.
Wealth!

*Enter a rich Lord and Lady on their way to the
wedding, lost. Pierre and Plug hide.*

Lord We must reach York by dawn. The wedding is
tomorrow!

Lady But where are we? This snow will make us all
blind.

Lord If Prince John should hear that Lord Falconbury
has failed to attend the royal wedding, I shudder to think
of his reaction.

*Pierre steps out from behind the tree. Plug steps out
also, looking scary.*

Pierre Your money or your life. (*To us.*) That sounded
good. I might use that again.

Lord Who are you?

Pierre Surely you recognise . . . Robin of Sherwood? And his hound of hell!

They wail in fear.

SCENE SEVEN

The snow falls harder. Jethro and Sarah in the forest. Freezing.

Jethro Snow's falling, Sarah. We'll have a white Christmas. We just have to . . . have to find some warmth. Find some shelter.

Sarah lies down.

No, don't sit down. We have to keep going. We'll find a village, there'll be a house, with a fire, and there'll be hot soup, Sarah, hot parsnip soup, with hot bread, they'll bake the bread fresh for us and we'll have beer! Beer and hot soup and hot, hot bread.

Sarah lies down again. The wind whistles. Jethro tries to pull her up.

Hot soup and hot bread. Hot soup.

Jethro also sits. The snow falls.

Hot soup. Hot soup.

They both fall and lie still. And suddenly through the snow can be seen a table, with hot soup and hot bread.

Hot soup. Hot soup! And hot bread! Sarah, get up. Sarah!

He pulls her up and they sit at the table in the middle of the snow.

And beer. Warm beer.

They eat and drink. They find warm clothes. They put them on. The Green Man enters. Jethro screams.

Green Man Do not be afraid.

Jethro Who are you?

Green Man I am the Green Man. I was born in the oak's sap. Its trunk is my core and the leaves are my fingers.

Jethro We are eating your food.

Green Man The food is what you asked for. At this time of year –

Jethro Christmas . . .

Green Man – I give to who is needy. Three wishes. This was your first. What is your second?

Jethro I want to see my father.

Out of the mist comes Jethro's father. He is dancing with a woman.

Who is he dancing with?

Green Man With your mother, of course. See how happy they are.

Jethro and Sarah stare.

Jethro Where are they?

Green Man In heaven.

Jethro With Jesus Christ?

Green Man With each other. And their ancestors.

They dance together. Then disappear.

Jethro Where are they going?

Green Man To the land beyond the forest where there are no trees and the sun never sets. You can go with them. Or you can live.

Pause. Jethro looks at Sarah.

Jethro I want to live.

Green Man Then what is your third wish?

Jethro I want her to speak again.

Green Man That is a wish I cannot grant. Only you can decide that fate.

Jethro What do you mean?

The Green Man disappears.

Did you hear that, Sarah? We have to keep going! It's up to us. It's up to us!

SCENE EIGHT

The camp. Robin and his men return.

Robin They're gone. Blood on the ground. Sign of a battle. Why did I leave them? John, Much, scour the forest. Find the children!

They leave.

Will Peter will look after them. We have to free Martin from the castle.

Robin I cannot think of that now. What have I done, Will?

Much and John return with Pierre's clothes.

Much No sign of the children. But we found this. Ripped. Bloody.

Little John Killed by a wolf most likely.

Pause.

Robin Then the children are dead too.

Pause.

I have been too strict in my ways. I have not cared for the weak. And now the weak have died. A woman would have told me not to leave them. A woman would have cared for them.

Will We can still save Martin, Robin. Good can come.

Robin Too late. Too late.

Will Robin.

John Robin! Shake off this melancholy!

Pause. Robin suddenly leaps up – and just in time, as the wounded Gisborne has appeared with his sword. Will ducks and Robin slashes at Gisborne. Gisborne and Robin fight and Robin cuts off his head.

Robin I know how we can get into the castle.

SCENE NINE

The castle.

Marion He sent Gisborne out?

Alice To kill the children. Oh, for a husband with such a taste for blood. Hubert is many things but an avenging angel he is not.

Marion Then they are dead already.

Alice Almost certainly. Why so pale? Oh look. Marion, come to the window! Look. Gisborne is returning on his stallion. I recognise his horsehair coat. And in his arms he carries the head of . . . oh, Marion . . .

Marion Of who?

Alice That foolish oaf must have tried to protect the children.

Marion Who, Alice? Who is it?

Alice Why, Robin Hood of course.

Marion faints.

Marion! The relief is too much for her. She has been kept hostage for so long by that brute.

Marion Robin! Robin!

Alice Wake up, Marion.

She pours water on her.

Marion Is he dead?

Alice Yes, my dear, your trials are over. He's dead! Do you want to see the body?

Marion I can't. Oh Robin. Robin!

Alice Guy's coming into the castle. Oh, I love a corpse.

Marion runs from the room.

Marion, where are you going?

Robin Hood in Gisborne's horsehide coat, with Gisborne's head on top, pretending to be Gisborne carrying Robin's head. He brings Much, Will, Little John in chains. Alice greets him.

Robin I am Guy of Gisborne. I return from the woods with a true prize. The head of the bandit. And in chains his merry men. Call the Prince!

Alice Prince John! Guy of Gisborne has returned from the forest.

Enter John.

John Guy, welcome home. You killed the children as I ordered?

Robin Yes, my lord.

John And disposed of them?

Robin My lord.

John And these are the merry men. We'll see how merry you feel after a few days in the dungeon.

Will I am looking forward to my stay, my lord.

John slaps Will.

John You look tired, Gisborne. Was the fight long?

Robin Not at all, my lord. Robin Hood was as you imagined, an untrained beast, no match for the refined skills of a soldier of your court.

John But why so pale? You look like a sheet.

Robin The night is cold, my lord. I feel my blood chill.

John Bring him wine! Food! Gisborne you are a faithful servant. Kneel before me.

Robin kneels.

I knight you Sir Guy of Gisborne and Sheriff of Nottingham. May these lands be for ever your domain.

Robin I shall obey you as long as I live.

John Put these men in the dungeon. Manacle them, give them an open wound and let the rats go to work. Feast well, Guy. I must sleep. I have a wedding to look forward to.

John leaves. Marion appears. Sees the dead body she thinks is Robin.

Marion Then it is true. He is dead.

Robin He is dead, my lady. Lady Alice, leave us. I will take these scoundrels to the dungeon.

Alice Yes, Guy.

Robin Sir Guy.

Alice Yes, Sir Guy.

Exit Alice.

Marion Show me his face.

Robin turns and Marion looks at the apparently dead Robin. Who then speaks.

Robin Why so sad, madam?

Marion screams. Robin smiles. He reveals the head of Guy.

Did you doubt me?

She slaps him.

Why do I deserve that?

Marion You frightened me. Oh, you are alive. You're really alive.

She holds him. Pause. She stops holding him.

So . . .

Robin So . . .

Marion You are here to save Martin.

Robin Yes. Is he ready?

Marion No. Not quite. I wasn't expecting . . . I thought you were dead, so . . . I will fetch him now.

Robin Let me help you.

Marion No! I will bring him here.

She leaves. Robin unlocks the chains on his men. They bring out rope.

Much I think the princess holds a candle for you, sir.

Robin I didn't notice anything.

Little John I did. Blushed like a French tomato, she did.

Robin It's just the light.

Little John It must be, looks like you're blushing yourself.

Enter Marion, dressed as Martin.

Robin Martin! We have come to deliver you from your chains. Where is Marion?

Marion She said you had no further need of her.

Robin Of course. She's right. Of course she is. Well then – men. Let's go!

They move to the doors. But Robin does not move.

Marion Robin. What keeps you here?

Robin I need to say something to Marion. I will not see her again.

Will Chief, we don't have time for this.

Robin Where is she, Martin? Tell me.

Marion Who, Marion? She's . . . she's . . . My lord, we should go . . .

Robin Not until I see her one more time.

Marion You will see her again, my lord!

Robin How can I be sure?

Marion Trust me, you can be sure! Let's just go!

Robin No, I have to see her!

Marion All right then!

She is about to reveal herself. But then enter Alice.

Alice What's going on here?

Pause.

Robin Hood? Back from the dead! Trickery! Soldiers! Soldiers!!

Robin Silence her!

Soldiers enter. Ten of them. Robin and his men are overcome.

John What is going on here?

Alice Treachery, my lord! Villainy! Necromancy! They have revived the brigand with spells of witches!

John (*to Robin*) Trying to steal your way into the castle? To kidnap my future bride? You are a reckless man. Martin, explain yourself!

Marion My lord. I happened to be in the castle seeking news of my lost brother Pierre. I saw Robin Hood trying to reach the bedroom of Marion. I believe he was trying to capture her.

John Fetch Marion, ensure her safety.

Marion Let me go, my lord!

John Very well.

Exit Marion. John takes Robin's arm.

Have you been to Norfolk? I have a castle there. It has a dungeon a hundred feet beneath the earth. No light penetrates that darkness. I will keep you alive in there for as long as my marriage lasts. Every year, on the anniversary of my wedding, I will come and visit you. And cut off a piece of you. First your fingers. Then your toes, your ears. Your nose. There are so many parts of a human being. I will be an old man before I'm finished with you.

Enter Marion. She kneels.

Marion My lord and master.

John You are safe.

Marion Yes, my lord.

John This outlaw was trying to take you back to the forest.

Marion What will you do to him?

John I have not decided.

Marion Set him free. Let it be a blessing to God on our wedding day.

John slaps Marion.

John I have a better idea, Marion. You don't worry your pretty girl's head about matters way beyond your understanding and I'll decide how best to bless our marriage. It's time you knew a woman's place, my sweet. Return to your chamber. The wedding day is upon us.

Marion exits.

Take them to the keep, hang them in chains. And tomorrow send them to Norfolk.

End of Act Four.

Act Five

SCENE ONE

*York. Jethro and Sarah arrive in York. The cathedral
bells ring out for the wedding day.*

Jethro This is York, Sarah, we need to get to the castle.
We must help Robin rescue Martin.

Sarah shakes her head. Goes the other way.

Sarah, where are you going? Sarah!

He goes after her.
    *Enter Pierre and Plug. Pierre dressed in Falconbury's
clothes.*

Pierre (*aside to us*) I cannot find the children anywhere!
And it's the morning of the wedding. My poor mistress
is due to marry that heathen. And once she is married
there is no way back for her! I have to stop it! I have to!
Oh, listen to those bells. Poor sweet Marion! What do
I do, Plug? Help me!

Plug just looks at him. Pierre looks up at the castle.

The drawbridge is coming down. Who is coming? Marion!

*John and Marion cross the stage on the way to the
wedding. He is waving to the crowds. She is not.
Head down. Frozen in distress.*

John Smile, Marion. It's our wedding day. Wave to the
crowds.

She does not move.

Marion, I need to tell you something. This morning I
sent soldiers to one hundred villages all over my future

86

kingdom. In each village they have arrested one boy and one girl. Should you fail to do your duty today, they have orders to hang all of those children. One hundred Jethros. One hundred Sarahs. And all because of you.

Now smile. And wave.

Pause. She smiles. And waves. The procession continues.

Pierre Oh Marion! How can I help you?!

Hold on, Plug. There's more coming. It's Robin! In chains. Is all hope lost?

Robin and his men, chained, are led in by three Soldiers.

Soldier Get into the cart!

Pierre Good morning, soldier. Do you know me?

Soldier No, sir.

Pierre I am Lord Falconbury, friend to Prince John and attendant to his wedding. This is my faithful aristocratic dog Rupert.

Plug barks aristocratically.

Now, tell me! What is this man's crime?

Soldier Treason, sir. This is Robin Hood.

Pierre A notorious scoundrel and swine.

He slaps Robin with his glove.

And where are you taking him?

Soldier To Norfolk, sir.

Pierre To the Prince's private dungeon. Quite right.

He slaps Robin again.

And what will you do to him there?

Soldier Torture him beyond all pain, sir.

Pierre Excellent!

He slaps Robin again.

This man robbed me a year back, stripped me and my wife bare of all our wealth. No tortures are great enough for such a scoundrel. In fact let me have a moment with him myself, I'll get the ball rolling.

Soldier Well, sir, it's not considered normal procedure.

Pierre Just this once. It's the royal wedding, after all.

Soldier What do you want to do to him?

Pierre Hand me that sword and I'll show you.

He gets the sword and smashes the hilt down on Robin.

Not heavy enough! Hand me that crossbow!

He gets the crossbow, smashes it on Robin.

Not heavy enough! Hand me that blunderbuss!

He grabs the blunderbuss and points it at the Soldiers.

And now hand Rupert the keys. And hurry up! We have a wedding to interrupt.

SCENE TWO

Music. We are in York Minster. Incense. Music.
Jethro and Sarah enter the cathedral (in the audience possibly).

Jethro Sarah, why have you led me to the cathedral? We should be trying to find Robin!

She makes her way to a seat.

Where are you going? Sarah!

Prince John arrives. Enters the cathedral. Then music strikes up. Singing.

Marion arrives in the cathedral. Soldiers all round her.

Marion approaches the altar. Prince John awaits her.

Bishop We are gathered here today to witness the union of Prince John, Prince Regent, Lord of Nottingham, Earl of Shaftesbury and Marion, Duchess of York, in holy matrimony before the eyes of God.

> *Beati omnes qui timent Dominum: qui ambulant in viis eius.*
> *Labores manuum tuarum quia manducabis: beatus es, et bene tibi erit.*
> *Uxor tua sicut vitis abundans in lateribus domus tuae.*
> *Filii tui sicut novellae olivarum in circuitu mensae tuae.*
> *Ecce sic benedicetur homo qui timet Dominum.*
> *Gloria Patri, et Filii in vita eternae.*
> *Kyrie eleison, Christe eleison, Kyrie eleison.*

Music.

Do you, John, son of Henry, Prince Regent, Earl of Sherbourne and Duke of Nottingham, accept this woman Marion as your lawful wife before God, cleansed of mortal sin, to honour and cherish until death do you part?

John I do.

Bishop Do you, Marion, daughter of Philip, Duke of York, accept this man John as your lord before God, cleansed of mortal sin, to honour, serve and obey him until death do you part?

Pause.

John Marion? (*Pause.*) Remember the children.

Marion I do.

Bishop Present the rings.

The rings are brought forward.

If any man or woman knows of any reason why this marriage should not be lawful before God let them speak now or for ever hold their peace.

Pause. Sarah tries to speak.

What was that?

John It was nothing. Continue with the ceremony. Give us the rings!

Sarah I know!

Pause.

Soldier Who speaks there?

Jethro Sarah?

Sarah I know!

Bishop Who is that who speaks?

John It's some stupid girl! Ignore her. Get her out of the church!

Sarah She cannot marry him. For her heart is already set on another.

John Another?

Bishop Bring her up here! Let us all look at her.

Jethro Sarah, what are you doing?

Sarah is brought to the altar.

Bishop What did you say?

Sarah She loves another.

John Who?! Who does she love more than me?

Sarah Robin Hood.

Jethro My lord, she does not know what she says.

Sarah I heard her in the forest.

John I know who you are. This child is a liar and apostate! She is the daughter of Robert Summers! She is heir to the devil himself, has welcomed Satan into her arms. Soldiers, take her!

Soldiers enter. Helmeted.

Soldiers My lord!

John Take this child to the river and drown her, for she is the devil's kin!

Jethro NO!

John Take her, I say. And her brother! Take them both!

Soldier Just one question, my lord!

Pause.

Is she the devil's kin? Or is she the daughter of the man you murdered?

John How dare you question me? Your name, sir!

Robin My name is Robin Hood.

The soldier unveils. It is Robin. Pause.

Sarah That's the man she's in love with!

Pause.

John Arrest them!

Real Soldiers enter. A fight in the cathedral. Makepeace helps Robin, but is killed. Alice helps John, but is chased by Marion and falls upside down into the font. Robin saves Marion's life and Pierre fights bravely, as does Jethro. The Soldiers are all killed. John is left pinioned on a cross in the cathedral.

Mercy!

Robin You would have sent me to a life of pain in a dripping dungeon. What mercy do I owe you now? You coward, you torturer, you murderer!

Marion Robin, show him mercy.

Robin Why?

Marion Because it is the plea of the woman who loves you.

Pause.

Robin You do love me?

Marion From the moment I saw you.

Robin Even though I was heartless?

Marion Even then I saw the heart inside you.

They kiss. Enter the Duke of York. Armed, with soldiers.

Duke of York Stop this wedding! Get away from my daughter, sir!

Marion Father!

Duke of York I arrest you, Prince John, and charge you with capital treason against King Richard the Lionheart, King of Aquitaine and England.

Pause.

You are not Prince John.

Robin No, my lord. He's up there.

John Duke, I welcome you home and command you to arrest these men.

Duke of York It's you I'll arrest, sir. For fomenting rebellion in our land. Take him away.

John I'll have my revenge on every one of you. I'll be king one day. And then, my friends . . . there will be bonfires.

He is led off.

Duke of York Who are you, sir?

Robin My name is Robin Hood.

Duke of York The brigand?

Robin Once a brigand. No more.

Duke of York You have stolen and killed for pleasure.

Robin I did, sir. Until I met your daughter.

Marion He saved me from the clutches of the Prince. Without him, and these children, I would have signed my fate before God. To marry a man I hate.

Pause.

Duke of York Then we shall forgive him and let him return to the forest.

Marion But I love him, Father.

Pause.

Duke of York He is a wild man, a bandit. Not fit for a duke's daughter.

Marion I love not titles nor positions.

Duke of York What is your blood?

Robin Common as the ground I sleep on.

Duke of York He is not even a yeoman.

Marion He is in my heart.

Duke of York And is she in yours?

Robin She is burnt there like a brand.

Pause.

Duke of York Then I welcome you as my own son into my house. But how did you defeat this wretched brother?

Robin By working together, my lord. Myself, my men, these children, Marion, and Martin of Sherwood.

Duke of York Martin of Sherwood?

Robin Marion, I had quite forgotten him. We have to find Martin, thank him . . . he and his sidekick Big Peter.

Duke of York Big Peter?

Marion My lord . . .

Robin A man of honest birth, Martin of Sherwood helped us, rescued the children, changed me and my ways. He is imprisoned in your castle. He must be honoured.

Marion Robin. Do you believe in miracles?

Robin I do now.

Marion Then hold your faith and I will bring Martin to you. Lord Falconbury, I will need your help.

Pierre But of course.

She exits.

Duke of York Martin of Sherwood? I have never heard of this man.

Robin When these children's father was killed for failing to pay the Holy Contribution, Martin and I saved them from death. But Martin was imprisoned in your dungeon. He is as fine a man as ever walked on greensward.

Marion enters as Martin but with the bridal dress still on.

Marion As fine a man?

Pause.

Much Marion . . . .

Will And Martin.

Little John Two souls in one body.

Robin It was you.

Pierre At last! And I, Pierre the unfunny clown, was Big Peter.

Sarah (*to Marion*) I knew it was you. I saw you in the forest.

Marion I am glad you did.

Jethro So Marion saved our lives?

Pierre And so did I.

Marion And Sarah saved mine.

Robin And the clown saved ours.

Pierre And Plug saved mine!

Duke of York And now I understand less than when I came. But this much I know. You love Robin. He loves you. And there is an altar free and a bishop ready to do some marrying.

Little John Marry her, Robin!

Much Marry her now in the cathedral!

Little John Let Jethro be page and Sarah maid of honour!

Will I shall hand the rings!

Much If I don't steal them first.

Duke of York I shall happily give away my daughter . . . to a good man.

Marion And I shall rejoice in the return of a father I love, and to be joined to a husband I adore.

Duke of York Lead them to the altar.

Robin No, my lord.

Pause.

Forgive me. But if I am to marry your daughter, the altar will not be made of marble and gold but of bark and branch. I cannot live in a castle of man with servants at my command and villages in my thrall. I live bound only to the beating of my heart. And that of the woman I love. Marion, come and wed me in the only cathedral I know.

Pause.

Duke of York Marion?

Marion The wood is what brought us together. Who else could marry us but the trees?

Duke of York Then let us to the forest!

They leave.

Alice (*from inside the font*) What about me? Don't leave me here! Hubert! Hubert!

EPILOGUE

The forest. Pierre there once again.

Pierre And that's how it came to be. That I found my heart in a wood of oak. And how Robin Hood found his.

Robin and Marion are high in the oak tree. Married, joined in the wood of the oak, surrounded by the children and the merry men . . .

The End.